Death

A Comedy in One Act

by Woody Allen

A Samuel French Acting Edition

New York Hollywood London Toronto
SAMUELFRENCH.COM

Copyright © 1975 by Woody Allen

ALL RIGHTS RESERVED

CAUTION: Professionals and amateurs are hereby warned that *DEATH* is subject to a Licensing Fee. It is fully protected under the copyright laws of the United States of America, the British Commonwealth, including Canada, and all other countries of the Copyright Union. All rights, including professional, amateur, motion picture, recitation, lecturing, public reading, radio broadcasting, television and the rights of translation into foreign languages are strictly reserved. In its present form the play is dedicated to the reading public only.

The amateur live stage performance rights to *DEATH* are controlled exclusively by Samuel French, Inc., and licensing arrangements and performance licenses must be secured well in advance of presentation. PLEASE NOTE that amateur Licensing Fees are set upon application in accordance with your producing circumstances. When applying for a licensing quotation and a performance license please give us the number of performances intended, dates of production, your seating capacity and admission fee. Licensing Fees are payable one week before the opening performance of the play to Samuel French, Inc., at 45 W. 25th Street, New York, NY 10010.

Licensing Fee of the required amount must be paid whether the play is presented for charity or gain and whether or not admission is charged.

Stock licensing fees quoted upon application to Samuel French, Inc.

For all other rights than those stipulated above, apply to: Rollins & Joffe, Inc., 130 West 57th Street, New York, NY 10019.

Particular emphasis is laid on the question of amateur or professional readings, permission and terms for which must be secured in writing from Samuel French, Inc.

Copying from this book in whole or in part is strictly forbidden by law, and the right of performance is not transferable.

Whenever the play is produced the following notice must appear on all programs, printing and advertising for the play: "Produced by special arrangement with Samuel French, Inc."

Due authorship credit must be given on all programs, printing and advertising for the play.

No one shall commit or authorize any act or omission by which the copyright of, or the right to copyright, this play may be impaired.
No one shall make any changes in this play for the purpose of production.
Publication of this play does not imply availability for performance. Both amateurs and professionals considering a production are strongly advised in their own interests to apply to Samuel French, Inc., for written permission before starting rehearsals, advertising, or booking a theatre.
No part of this book may be reproduced, stored in a retrieval system, or transmitted in any form, by any means, now known or yet to be invented, including mechanical, electronic, photocopying, recording, videotaping, or otherwise, without the prior written permission of the publisher.

ISBN 978-0-573-62129-1   Printed in U.S.A.   #52

CAST

(In Order of Appearance)

    KLEINMAN

    HANK

    AL

    SAM

    HACKER

    JOHN

    VICTOR

    ANNA

    DOCTOR

    GINA

    MAN

    COP (POLICEMAN)

    BILL

    FRANK

    DON

    HENRY

    ASSISTANT

    SPIRO

    ABE

    MANIAC

The curtain rises on KLEINMAN, asleep in his bed at two A.M. There is a pounding at the door. Finally, and with great effort and determination, he gets up.

KLEINMAN

Huh?

VOICES

Open up! Hey—come on, we know you're there! Open up! Let's go, open! . . .

KLEINMAN

Huh? What?

VOICES

Let's go, open up!

KLEINMAN

What? Wait! *(Turns on the light)* Who's there?

VOICES

Come on, open up! Let's go!

KLEINMAN

Who is it?

VOICE

Let's go, Kleinman—hurry.

KLEINMAN

Hacker—that's Hacker's voice. Hacker?

VOICE

Kleinman, will you open up?!

KLEINMAN

I'm coming, I'm coming. I was asleep—wait! *(All with stumbling and great effort and clumsiness. He looks at the clock)* My God, it's two-thirty . . . Coming, wait a minute! *(He opens the door and a half-dozen men enter)*

HANK

For God's sake, Kleinman, are you deaf?

KLEINMAN

I was asleep. It's two-thirty. What's going on?

AL

We need you. Get dressed.

KLEINMAN

What?

SAM

Let's go, Kleinman. We don't have forever.

KLEINMAN

What is this?

AL

Come on, move.

KLEINMAN

Move where? Hacker, it's the middle of the night.

HACKER

Well, wake up.

KLEINMAN

What's going on?

JOHN

Don't play ignorant.

KLEINMAN

Who's playing ignorant? I was in a deep sleep. What do you think I was doing two-thirty in the morning—dancing?

HACKER

We need every available man.

KLEINMAN

For what?

VICTOR

What's wrong with you, Kleinman? Where have you been that you don't know what's going on?

KLEINMAN

What are you talking about?

AL

Vigilantes.

KLEINMAN

What?

AL

Vigilantes.

JOHN

But with a plan this time.

HACKER

And well worked out.

SAM

A great plan.

KLEINMAN

Er, does anybody want to tell me why you're here? Because I'm cold in my underwear.

HACKER

Let's just say we need all the help we can get. Now get dressed.

DEATH

VICTOR
(Menacingly)

And hurry.

KLEINMAN

Okay, I'm getting dressed . . . May I please know what it's all about?
(He starts pulling on some trousers apprehensively)

JOHN

The killer's been spotted. By two women. They saw him entering the park.

KLEINMAN

What killer?

VICTOR

Kleinman, this is no time for babbling.

KLEINMAN

Who's babbling? What killer? You come barging in—I'm in a deep sleep—

HACKER

Richardson's killer—Jampel's killer.

AL

Mary Quilty's killer.

SAM

The maniac.

HANK

The strangler.

KLEINMAN

Which maniac? Which strangler?

JOHN

The same one who killed Eisler's boy and strangled Jensen with piano wire.

DEATH

KLEINMAN

Jensen? . . . The big night watchman?

HACKER

That's right. He took him from behind. Crept up quietly and slipped piano wire around his neck. He was blue when they found him. Saliva frozen down the corner of his mouth.

KLEINMAN
(Looks around the room)
Yeah, well, look, I have to go to work tomorrow—

VICTOR

Let's go, Kleinman. We've got to stop him before he strikes again.

Kleinman

We? We and me?

HACKER

The police can't seem to handle it.

KLEINMAN

Well, then we should write letters and complain. I'll get on it first thing in the morning.

HACKER

They're doing the best they can, Kleinman. They're baffled.

SAM

Everyone's baffled.

AL

Don't tell us you've heard nothing about all this?

JOHN

That's hard to believe.

KLEINMAN

Well, the truth is—it's the height of the season . . . We're busy . . . *(They're not buying his naïveté)* Don't even take a lunch hour—and I love to eat . . . Hacker'll tell you I love to eat.

                    HACKER
But this ghastly business has been going on for some time now. Don't you follow the news?

                    KLEINMAN
I don't get a chance.

                    HACKER
Everyone's terrified. People can't walk the streets at night.

                    JOHN
Streets nothing. The Simon sisters were killed in their own home because they didn't lock the door. Throats cut ear to ear.

                    KLEINMAN
I thought you said he's a strangler.

                    JOHN
Kleinman, don't be naïve.

                    KLEINMAN
N–now that you mention it, I could use a new lock on this door.

                    HACKER
It's horrible. No one knows when he'll strike next.

                    KLEINMAN
When did it start? I don't know why I wasn't told anything.

                    HACKER
First one body, then another, then more. The city's in a panic. Everyone but you.

                    KLEINMAN
Well, you can relax, because now I'm in a panic.

HACKER
It's difficult in the case of a madman because there's no motive. Nothing to go on.

KLEINMAN
No one's been robbed or raped or—tickled a little?

VICTOR
Only strangled.

KLEINMAN
Even Jensen . . . He's so powerful.

SAM
He *was* powerful. Right now, his tongue is sticking out and he's blue.

KLEINMAN
Blue . . . It's a bad color for a man of forty . . . And there's no clue? A hair—or a fingerprint?

HACKER
Yes. They found a hair.

KLEINMAN
So? All they need today is one hair. Put it under a microscope. One, two, three, they know the whole story. What color is it?

HACKER
Your color.

KLEINMAN
My—don't look at me . . . Nothing of mine's fallen out recently. I . . . Look, let's not get crazy . . . The trick is to remain logical.

HACKER
Uh-huh.

KLEINMAN
Sometimes there's a clue in the victims—like they're all nurses or they're all bald . . . or bald nurses . . .

JOHN
You tell us what the similarity is?

SAM
That's right. Between Eisler's boy and Mary Quilty and Jensen and Jampel—

KLEINMAN
If I knew more about the case . . .

AL
If he knew more about the case. There *is* no similarity. Except once they all were alive and now they're all dead. There's the thing in common.

HACKER
He's right. No one is safe, Kleinman. If that's what you're thinking.

AL
He probably wants to reassure himself!

JOHN
Yeah.

SAM
There is no pattern, Kleinman.

VICTOR
It's not just nurses.

AL
No one's immune.

KLEINMAN
I wasn't trying to reassure myself. I was asking a simple question.

SAM

Well, don't ask so many damn questions. We've got work to do.

VICTOR

We're all worried. Anyone can be next.

KLEINMAN

Look, I'm not good at these things. What do I know about a manhunt? I'll just be in the way. Let me make a cash donation. That'll be my contribution. Let me pledge a few dollars—

SAM
(Finding a hair by the bureau)

What's this?

KLEINMAN

What?

SAM

This? In your comb. It's a hair.

KLEINMAN

That's because I use it to comb my hair.

SAM

The color's identical with the hair found by the police.

KLEINMAN

Are you crazy? It's a black hair. There's a million of black hairs around. Why are you putting it in an envelope? Wha—it's a common thing. Here—*(Points to JOHN)* him— he's got black hair.

JOHN
(Grabs KLEINMAN)
What are you accusing me of, eh, Kleinman?!

KLEINMAN

Who's accusing!? He's got my hair in an envelope. Give me that hair back!
(Grabs the envelope, but JOHN pulls him off)

JOHN

Leave him alone!

SAM

I'm doing my duty.

VICTOR

He's right. The police have requested all citizens' help.

HACKER

Yes. Now we have a plan.

KLEINMAN

What kind of plan?

AL

We can count on you, can't we?

VICTOR

Oh, we can count on Kleinman. He figures in the plan.

KLEINMAN

I do figure in the plan? So what's the plan?

JOHN

You'll be informed, don't worry.

KLEINMAN

He needs my hair in that envelope?

SAM

Just get your clothes on and meet us downstairs. And hurry up. We're wasting time.

KLEINMAN

Okay, but give me a hint what the plan is like?

HACKER
Hurry, Kleinman, for God's sake. This is a matter of life and death. You better dress warm. It's cold out there.

KLEINMAN
Okay, okay . . . just tell me the plan. If I know the plan I can think about it.
(But they go, leaving KLEINMAN to dress with a nervous clumsiness)

KLEINMAN
Where the hell's my shoehorn? . . . This is ridiculous . . . wake a man up in the middle of the night and with such horrible news. What are we paying a police force for? One minute I'm curled up asleep in a nice warm bed and the next I'm involved in some plan, a homicidal maniac who comes up behind you and—

ANNA
(An old battle-ax, enters with candle, unseen, surprising KLEINMAN) Kleinman?

KLEINMAN
(Turning, frightened out of his wits)
Who's that!!?

ANNA
What?

KLEINMAN
For God's sake, don't creep up on me like that!

ANNA
I heard voices.

KLEINMAN
Some men were here. All of a sudden I'm on a vigilante committee.

ANNA
Now?

KLEINMAN
Apparently there's a killer loose—it can't wait for the morning. He's a night owl.

ANNA
Oh, the maniac.

KLEINMAN
So if you knew about it, why didn't you tell me?

ANNA
Because everytime I try and talk to you about it you don't want to hear.

KLEINMAN
Who doesn't?

ANNA
You're always too busy with work—and your hobbies.

KLEINMAN
Do you mind if it's the height of the season?

ANNA
I said to you there's an unsolved murder, there's two unsolved murders, there's six unsolved murders—and all you say is, "Later, later."

KLEINMAN
Because the times you pick to tell me.

ANNA
Yeah?

KLEINMAN
My birthday party. So I'm having a good time, I'm opening presents, so you creep up to me with that long face and say, "Did you read in the paper? A girl got her throat cut?" You couldn't pick a more appropriate time? A man has a little fun—enter the voice of doom.

ANNA
Unless it's something nice, no time is appropriate.

KLEINMAN
Meanwhile, where's my tie?

ANNA
What do you need a tie for? You're going to hunt a maniac?

KLEINMAN
Do you mind?

ANNA
What is it, a formal hunt?

KLEINMAN
Do I know who I'm going to meet? What if my boss is down there?

ANNA
I'm sure he's dressed casually.

KLEINMAN
Look who they're enlisting to track down a killer. I'm a salesman.

ANNA
Don't let him get behind you.

KLEINMAN
Thanks, Anna, I'll tell him you said to keep in front.

ANNA
Well, you don't have to be so nasty. He's got to be caught.

KLEINMAN
Then let the police catch him. I'm scared to go down there. It's cold and dark.

ANNA
Be a man for once in your life.

KLEINMAN

That's easy for you to say, because you're going back to bed.

ANNA

And what if he should find his way to this house and come in a window?

KLEINMAN

Then you got problems.

ANNA

If I'm attacked, I'll blow pepper on him.

KLEINMAN

Blow what?

ANNA

I sleep with a little pepper near the bed, and if he comes near me I'll blow pepper in his eyes.

KLEINMAN

Good thinking, Anna. Believe me, if he gets in here, you and your pepper will be on the ceiling.

ANNA

I'm keeping everything double-locked.

KLEINMAN

Hm, maybe I better take some pepper.

ANNA

Take this.
(She hands him a charm)

KLEINMAN

What's this?

ANNA

A charm that wards off evil. I bought it from a crippled beggar.

KLEINMAN
(Looks at it, unimpressed)
Right. Just give me some pepper.

ANNA
Oh, don't worry. You won't be alone down there.

KLEINMAN
That's true. They've got a very clever plan.

ANNA
What?

KLEINMAN
I don't know yet.

ANNA
So how do you know it's so clever?

KLEINMAN
Because these are the best minds in town. Believe me, they know what they're doing.

ANNA
I hope so, for your sake.

KLEINMAN
All right, keep the door locked and don't open it for anyone—not even me, unless I happen to be screaming, "Open the door!" Then open it quickly.

ANNA
Good luck, Kleinman.

KLEINMAN
(Takes a look out his window into the black night)
Look at it out there . . . It's so black . . .

ANNA
I don't see anybody.

KLEINMAN

Me neither. You'd figure there'd be groups of citizens with torches or something—

ANNA

Well, as long as they've got a plan.
(Pause)

KLEINMAN

Anna—

ANNA

Yes?

KLEINMAN
(Looking into the black)
Do you ever think of dying?

ANNA

Why should I think of dying? Why, do you?

KLEINMAN

Not usually, but when I do, it's not by being strangled or having my throat cut.

ANNA

I should hope not.

KLEINMAN

I think of dying in a nicer way.

ANNA

Believe me, there's plenty of nicer ways.

KLEINMAN

Like what?

ANNA

Like what? You're asking me a nice way to die?

KLEINMAN

Yeah.

DEATH

ANNA

I'm thinking.

KLEINMAN

Yeah.

ANNA

Poison.

KLEINMAN

Poison? That's terrible.

ANNA

Why?

KLEINMAN

Are you joking? You get cramps.

ANNA

Not necessarily.

KLEINMAN

Do you know what you're talking about?

ANNA

Potassium cyanide.

KLEINMAN

Oh . . . my expert. You're not catching me with poison. You know what it is even if you eat a bad clam?

ANNA

That's not poison. That's food poisoning.

KLEINMAN

Who wants to swallow anything?

ANNA

So how do you want to die?

KLEINMAN

Old age. Many years in the future. When I'm through the

long journey of life. Surrounded in a comfortable bed by relatives—when I'm ninety.

ANNA

But that's just a dream. Obviously, at any second you could get your neck snapped in two by a homicidal killer—or your throat cut . . . not when you're ninety, right now.

KLEINMAN

It's so comforting to discuss these things with you, Anna.

ANNA

Well, I'm worried about you. Look at it down there. There's a killer loose and plenty of places to hide on such a black night—alleys, doorways, under the railroad overpass . . . You'd never see him in a dark shadow—a diseased mind, lurking in the night with piano wire—

KLEINMAN

You made your point—I'm going back to bed!
(Knock on door and voice)

VOICE

Let's go, Kleinman!

KLEINMAN

I'm coming, I'm coming. *(Kisses ANNA)* See you later.

ANNA

Look where you're going.
(He goes out, joining AL, who has been left to see that he gets things straight)

KLEINMAN

I don't know why this is suddenly my responsibility.

AL

We're all in it together.

DEATH

KLEINMAN
It'll be just my luck, I'll be the one to find him. Oh, I forgot my pepper!

AL
What?

KLEINMAN
Hey, where is everybody?

AL
They had to move on. Correct timing is urgent in bringing the plan off.

KLEINMAN
So what is this great plan?

AL
You'll find out.

KLEINMAN
When are you going to tell me? After he's captured?

AL
Don't be so impatient.

KLEINMAN
Look—it's late, and I'm cold. Not to mention nervous.

AL
Hacker and the others had to leave, but he said to tell you you'll receive word as soon as possible as to how you fit in.

KLEINMAN
Hacker said that?

AL
Yes.

KLEINMAN
So what do I do, now that I'm out of my room and my warm bed?

AL

You wait.

KLEINMAN

For what?

AL

For word.

KLEINMAN

What word?

AL

Word of how you fit in.

KLEINMAN

I'm going back home.

AL

No! Don't you dare. A wrong move at this point could endanger all our lives. You think I want to wind up a corpse?

KLEINMAN

So tell me the plan.

AL

I can't tell you.

KLEINMAN

Why not?

AL

Because I don't know it.

KLEINMAN

Look, it's a cold night—-

AL

Each of us only knows one small fraction of the overall plan at any given moment—his own assignment—and no one is allowed to disclose his function to another. It's a precaution against the maniac finding out the plan. If each man properly brings off his own part, then the whole scheme will be brought to a successful conclusion. In the meantime, the plan can't be either carelessly disclosed or given up under duress or threat. Each one can only account for a tiny fragment which would have no meaning to the maniac should he gain access to it. Clever?

KLEINMAN
Brilliant. I don't know what's going on and I'm going home.

AL
I can't say any more. Suppose it was you who killed all those people?

KLEINMAN
Me?

AL
The killer might be any of us.

KLEINMAN
Well, it's not me. I don't go around hacking people to death at the height of the season.

AL
I'm sorry, Kleinman.

KLEINMAN
So what do I do? What's my assignment?

AL
If I were you I would try and contribute as best I could until my function became clearer.

KLEINMAN
Contribute how?

AL
It's hard to be specific.

KLEINMAN

Can you give me a hint? Because I'm beginning to feel like a fool.

AL

Things may seem chaotic but they're not.

KLEINMAN

But there was such a rush to get me out here. Now I'm here and ready and everybody's gone.

AL

I have to go.

KLEINMAN

So what was so urgent? . . . Go? What do you mean?

AL

My work is finished here. I'm due elsewhere.

KLEINMAN

That means I'll be out here on the street myself.

AL

Perhaps.

KLEINMAN

Perhaps nothing. If we're together and you leave, I'm alone. That's arithmetic.

AL

Be careful.

KLEINMAN

Oh, no, I'm not staying here alone! You gotta be kidding! There's a madman walking around loose! I don't get along with madmen! I'm a very logical guy.

AL

The plan doesn't allow for us to be together.

KLEINMAN
Look, let's not make it into a romance. *We* don't have to be together. Me and any twelve strong men will do.

AL
I must go.

KLEINMAN
I don't want to be here alone. I'm serious.

AL
Just be careful.

KLEINMAN
Look, my hand is shaking—and you haven't left yet! You go and my whole body'll shake.

AL
Kleinman, other lives are dependent on you. Don't fail us.

KLEINMAN
You shouldn't count on me. I have a great fear of death! I'd rather do almost anything else than die!

AL
Good luck.

KLEINMAN
And what about the maniac? Is there any further news? Has he been spotted again?

AL
The police saw a large, terrifying figure lurking near the ice company. But no one really knows.
(Exits. We hear his footsteps going off softer and softer)

KLEINMAN
It's enough for me! I'll stay away from the ice company! *(Alone—wind sound effects)* Oh, boy, nothing like a night on the town. I don't know why I can't just wait in my room till I'm given a specific assignment. What was that noise!? The

wind—the wind is not too thrilling either. It could blow a sign down on me. Well, I've got to keep calm . . . People are counting on me . . . Keep my eyes open and if I see something suspicious I'll report it to the others . . . Except there are no others . . . I have to remember to make some more friends next chance I get . . . Maybe if I walked up a block or two I'll run into some of the others . . . How far could they have gotten? Unless this is what they want. Maybe this is part of the scheme. Maybe if anything dangerous happens, Hacker has me under some kind of surveillance where they'd all come to my aid . . . *(Laughs nervously)* I'm sure I haven't been left alone to wander the streets all by myself. They have to realize I'd be no match for a crazy killer. A maniac has the strength of ten and I have the strength of a half of one . . . Unless they're using me as a decoy . . . You think they'd do that? Leave me out here like a lamb? . . . The killer pounces on me and they come bursting out quickly and grab him—unless they come bursting out slowly . . . I never had a strong neck. *(A black figure runs across background)* What was that? Maybe I should go back . . . I'm starting to get far from where I started . . . How are they going to find me to assign me my instructions? Not only that, but I'm going toward a part of the city which is unfamiliar to me . . . then what? Yeah—maybe I better turn around and retrace my steps before I become good and lost . . . *(He hears slow, menacing steps coming toward him)* Uh-oh . . . That's footsteps—the maniac probably has feet . . . Oh, God, save me . . .

DOCTOR

Kleinman, is that you?

KLEINMAN

What? Who is it?

DOCTOR

It's just the doctor.

DEATH

KLEINMAN

You gave me a scare. Tell me, have you heard anything from Hacker or any of the others?

DOCTOR

Concerning your participation?

KLEINMAN

Yes. Time is being wasted and I'm wandering around like a jackass. I mean, I'm keeping my eyes open, but if I knew what I was supposed to be doing—

DOCTOR

Hacker did mention something about you.

KLEINMAN

What?

DOCTOR

I can't remember.

KLEINMAN

Great. I'm the forgotten man.

DOCTOR

I think I heard him say something. I'm not sure.

KLEINMAN

Look, why don't we patrol together? In case there's trouble.

DOCTOR

I can only walk along a little way with you. Then I have other business.

KLEINMAN

It's funny to see a doctor up in the middle of the night . . . I know how you guys hate to make house calls. Ha-ha-ha-ha. *(No laugh)* It's a very cold night . . . *(Nothing)* You, er—you think we'll spot him tonight? *(Nothing)* I suppose you have an important function to carry out in the plan? See, I don't know mine yet.

DOCTOR

My interest is purely scientific.

KLEINMAN

I'm sure.

DOCTOR

Here is a chance to learn something about the nature of his insanity. Why is he the way he is? What goads someone toward such a type of antisocial behavior? Are there some other unusual qualities about him? Sometimes the very impulses that cause a maniac to murder inspire him to highly creative ends. It's a very complex phenomenon. Also, I would like to know if he has been mad from birth or if his madness is caused by some disease or accident that has damaged his brain or from the accumulated stress of adverse circumstances. There are a million facts to learn. For instance: Why does he choose to express his impulses in the act of murder? Does he do it of his own will or does he imagine he hears voices? You know at one time the mad were considered to be divinely inspired. All this is worth examining for the record.

KLEINMAN

Sure, but first we have to catch him.

DOCTOR

Yes, Kleinman, if I have my way, I will be left alone to study this creature scrupulously, dissecting him down to the last chromosome. I would like to put his every cell under a microscope. See what he's composed of. Analyze his juices. Break down the blood, probe the brain minutely, until I had a one hundred percent understanding of precisely what he is in every aspect.

KLEINMAN

Can you ever really know a person? I mean, know him—not know about him, but know—I mean, actually know him—where you know him—I'm talking about knowing a person—you know what I mean by knowing? Knowing. Really knowing. To know. Know. To know.

DOCTOR

Kleinman, you're an idiot.

KLEINMAN

Do you understand what I'm saying?

DOCTOR

You do your job and I'll do mine.

KLEINMAN

I don't know my job.

DOCTOR

Then don't criticize.

KLEINMAN

Who's criticizing? *(A scream is heard. They start)* What was that?

DOCTOR

Do you hear footsteps behind us?

KLEINMAN

I've been hearing footsteps behind me since I was eight years old.

(Scream again)

DOCTOR

Someone's coming.

KLEINMAN

Maybe he didn't like all that talk about dissecting him.

DOCTOR

You'd better get out of here, Kleinman.

KLEINMAN

My pleasure.

DOCTOR

Quick! This way!
(Noise of someone approaching heavily)

KLEINMAN

That alley's a dead end.

DOCTOR

I know what I'm doing!

KLEINMAN

Yeah, but we'll be trapped and killed!

DOCTOR

Are you going to argue with me? I'm a doctor.

KLEINMAN

But I know that alley—it's a dead end. There's no way of getting out!

DOCTOR

Goodbye, Kleinman. Do what you want!
(He runs up the dead end)

KLEINMAN
(Calling after him)
Wait—I'm sorry! *(Noise of someone approaching)* I've got to stay calm! Do I run or do I hide? I'll run and hide! *(He runs and bumps into a young WOMAN)* Oooof!

GINA

Oh!

KLEINMAN

Who are you?

GINA

Who are you?

KLEINMAN

Kleinman. Did you hear screams?

GINA

Yes, and I got scared. I don't know where they were coming from.

KLEINMAN

It doesn't matter. The main thing is that they were screams, and screams are never any good.

GINA

I'm frightened!

KLEINMAN

Let's get out of here!

GINA

I can't go too far. I have something to do.

KLEINMAN

You're in on the plan too?

GINA

Aren't you?

KLEINMAN

Not yet. I can't seem to find out what I should be doing. You haven't heard anything about me by any chance?

GINA

You're Kleinman.

KLEINMAN

Exactly.

GINA

I heard something about a Kleinman. I don't remember what.

KLEINMAN

You know where Hacker is?

GINA

Hacker was murdered.

KLEINMAN
What!?

GINA
I think it was Hacker.

KLEINMAN
Hacker's dead?

GINA
I'm not sure if they said Hacker or someone else.

KLEINMAN
Nobody's sure of anything! Nobody knows anything! This is some plan! We're dropping like flies!

GINA
Maybe it wasn't Hacker.

KLEINMAN
Let's get away from here. I wandered away from where I should have been, and they're probably looking for me, and with my luck, they'll blame me if the plan fails.

GINA
I can't remember who's dead. Hacker or Maxwell.

KLEINMAN
I'll tell you the truth, it's hard to keep track. And what's a young woman like yourself doing out on the streets? This is a man's work.

GINA
I'm used to the streets at night.

KLEINMAN
Oh?

GINA
Well, I'm a prostitute.

KLEINMAN
No kidding. Gee, I never met one before . . . I thought you'd be taller.

GINA
I didn't embarrass you, did I?

KLEINMAN
To tell you the truth, I'm very provincial.

GINA
Yes?

KLEINMAN
I, er—I'm never even up at this hour. I mean *never*. It's the middle of the night. Unless I'm sick or something—but barring extreme nausea I sleep like a baby.

GINA
Well, you're out on a clear night anyhow.

KLEINMAN
Yes.

GINA
You can see a lot of stars.

KLEINMAN
Actually, I'm very nervous. I'd prefer to be home in bed. It's weird at night. All the stores are closed. There's no traffic. You can jaywalk . . . No one stops you . . .

GINA
Well, that's good, isn't it?

KLEINMAN
Er—it's a funny feeling. There's no civilization . . . I could take my pants off and run naked down the main street.

GINA
Uh-huh.

KLEINMAN

I mean, I wouldn't. But I could.

GINA

To me the city at night is so cold and dark and empty. This must be what it's like in outer space.

KLEINMAN

I never cared for outer space.

GINA

But you're in outer space. We're just this big, round ball floating in space . . . You can't tell which way is up.

KLEINMAN

You think that's good? I'm a man who likes to know which way is up and which way is down and where's the bathroom.

GINA

You think there's life on any of those billions of stars out there?

KLEINMAN

I personally don't know. Although I hear there may be life on Mars, but the guy that told me is only in the hosiery business.

GINA

And it all goes on forever.

KLEINMAN

How can it go on forever? Sooner or later it must stop. Right? I mean sooner or later it must end and there's, er—a wall or something—be logical.

GINA

Are you saying the universe is finite?

KLEINMAN

I'm not saying anything. I don't want to get involved. I want to know what I'm supposed to be doing.

GINA
(Pointing it out)
There, you can see Gemini . . . the twins . . . and Orion the hunter . . .

KLEINMAN
Where do you see twins? They hardly look alike.

GINA
Look at that tiny star out there . . . all alone. You can barely see it.

KLEINMAN
You know how far that must be? I'd hate to tell you.

GINA
We're seeing the light that left that star millions of years ago. It's just now reaching us.

KLEINMAN
I know what you mean.

GINA
Did you know that light travels 186,000 miles per second?

KLEINMAN
That's too fast if you ask me. I like to enjoy a thing. There's no leisure any more.

GINA
For all we know that star disappeared millions of years ago and it's taken that light, traveling 186,000 miles a second, millions of years to reach us.

KLEINMAN
You're saying that star may not still be out there?

GINA
That's right.

KLEINMAN
Even though I see it with my own eyes?

GINA

That's right.

KLEINMAN

That's very scary, because if I see something with my own eyes, I like to think it's there. I mean, if that's true, they could all be like that—all burnt out—but we're just late getting the news.

GINA

Kleinman, who knows what's real?

KLEINMAN

What's real is what you can touch with your hands.

GINA

Oh? *(He kisses her; she responds passionately)* That'll be six dollars, please.

KLEINMAN

For what?

GINA

You had a little fun, didn't you?

KLEINMAN

A little, yes . . .

GINA

Well, I'm in business.

KLEINMAN

Yeah, but six dollars for a little kissing. For six dollars I could buy a muffler.

GINA

All right, give me five dollars.

KLEINMAN

Don't you ever kiss for nothing?

DEATH

GINA

Kleinman, this is business. For pleasure, I kiss women.

KLEINMAN

Women? What a coincidence . . . me too.

GINA

I've got to go.

KLEINMAN

I didn't mean to insult you—

GINA

You didn't. I have to go.

KLEINMAN

Will you be okay?

GINA

I have my assignment to carry out. Good luck. I hope you find what you're supposed to do.

KLEINMAN
(Calling after her)

I didn't mean to act like an animal—I'm really one of the nicest people I know! *(And he's alone as her footsteps die out)* Well, this has gone far enough. I'm going home and that's it. Except then tomorrow they'll come around and ask where I was. They'll say, the plan went wrong, Kleinman, and it's your fault. How is it my fault? What's the difference. They'll find a way. They'll need a scapegoat. That's probably my part of the plan. I'm always blamed when nothing works. I—*(He hears a moan)* What? Who's that!?

DOCTOR
(Crawls onto the stage, mortally wounded)

Kleinman—

KLEINMAN

Doctor!

DOCTOR

I'm dying.

KLEINMAN

I'll get a doctor . . .

DOCTOR

I am a doctor.

KLEINMAN

Yes, but you're a dying doctor.

DOCTOR

It's too late—he caught me . . . ugh . . . There was no place to run.

KLEINMAN

Help! Help! Somebody come quickly!

DOCTOR

Don't yell, Kleinman . . . You don't want the killer to find you.

KLEINMAN

Listen, I don't care any more! Help! *(Then, thinking he might be found by the killer, he softens his voice)* Help . . . Who is he? Did you get a good look at him?

DOCTOR

No, just suddenly, a stab in the back.

KLEINMAN

Too bad, he didn't stab you from the front. You might have seen him.

DOCTOR

I'm dying, Kleinman—

KLEINMAN

It's nothing personal.

DOCTOR

What kind of stupid thing is that to say.

KLEINMAN

What can I say? I'm just trying to make conversation—

(A MAN runs on)

MAN

What's happening? Did someone call for help?

KLEINMAN

The doctor's dying . . . Get help . . . Wait! Did you hear anything about me?

MAN

Who are you?

KLEINMAN

Kleinman.

MAN

Kleinman . . . Kleinman . . . Something, yes . . . They're looking for you . . . It's important . . .

KLEINMAN

Who is?

MAN

Something to do with your assignment.

KLEINMAN

Finally.

MAN

I'll tell them I saw you.

(Runs off)

DOCTOR

Kleinman, do you believe in reincarnation?

KLEINMAN

What's that?

DOCTOR

Reincarnation—that a person comes back to life again as something else.

KLEINMAN

Like what?

DOCTOR

Er . . . uh . . . another living thing . . .

KLEINMAN

What do you mean? Like an animal?

DOCTOR

Yes.

KLEINMAN

You mean like you may live again as a frog?

DOCTOR

Forget it, Kleinman, I didn't say anything.

KLEINMAN

Listen, anything's possible, but it's hard to imagine if a man is president of a big corporation in this life, that he'll wind up a chipmunk.

DOCTOR

It's getting black.

KLEINMAN

Look, why don't you tell me what your part in the plan is? Since you'll be out of commission, I could take it over, because so far I haven't been able to find out my assignment.

DOCTOR

My assignment wouldn't do you any good. I'm the only one who could carry it out.

KLEINMAN

For God's sake, I can't tell if we're too well organized or not organized enough.

DEATH

DOCTOR

Don't fail us, Kleinman. We need you.
(He dies)

KLEINMAN

Doctor? Doctor? Oh, my God . . . What do I do? The hell with it. I'm going home! Let 'em all run around all night like crackpots. The height of the season. No one'll tell me anything. I just don't want them to blame me for everything. Well, why should they blame me? I came when they called. They had nothing for me to do.
(A COP enters with the MAN who went looking for help)

MAN

Is there a dying man here?

KLEINMAN

I'm dying.

COP

You? What about him?

KLEINMAN

He's already dead.

COP

Were you a friend of his?

KLEINMAN

He took my tonsils out.
(COP kneels to inspect the body)

MAN

I was dead once.

KLEINMAN

Pardon me?

MAN

Dead: I've been dead. During the war. Wounded. There I lay on an operating table. Surgeons sweating to save my life. Suddenly they lost me—pulse stopped. It was all over. One of 'em, I'm told, had the presence of mind to massage my heart. Then it began beating again, so I lived, but for a tiny moment there, I was officially dead . . . According to science, too—dead . . . but that was a long time ago. That's why I can sympathize when I see one of these fellows.

KLEINMAN

So how was it?

MAN

What?

KLEINMAN

Being dead. Did you see anything?

MAN

No. It was just . . . nothing.

KLEINMAN

You don't remember any afterlife?

MAN

No.

KLEINMAN

My name didn't come up?

MAN

There was nothing. There is nothing after, Kleinman. Nothing.

KLEINMAN

I don't want to go. Not yet. Not now. I don't want what happened to him to happen to me. Trapped in an alley . . . stabbed . . . the others strangled . . . even Hacker . . . by this fiend.

MAN

Hacker wasn't murdered by the maniac.

KLEINMAN

No?

MAN

Hacker was assassinated by plotters.

KLEINMAN

Plotters?

MAN

The other faction.

KLEINMAN

What other faction?

MAN

You know about the other faction, don't you?

KLEINMAN

I don't know anything! I'm lost in the night.

MAN

Certain ones. Shepherd and Willis. They've always been at odds with Hacker's approach to the problem.

KLEINMAN

What?

MAN

Well, Hacker hasn't exactly gotten results.

KLEINMAN

Well, neither have the police.

POLICEMAN
(Rising)

We will, though. If the goddamn civilians would keep out of it.

KLEINMAN

I thought you wanted help.

POLICEMAN

Help, yes. Not a lot of confusion and panic. But don't worry. We've got a couple of clues and we're running data through our computers. These babies are the best electronic brains. Incapable of error. Let's see how long he holds out against them.

(Kneels)

KLEINMAN

So who killed Hacker?

POLICEMAN

There's a faction that opposes Hacker.

KLEINMAN

Who? Shepherd and Willis?

POLICEMAN

Plenty have defected to their side. Believe me. I even heard a group has splintered off from the new group.

KLEINMAN

Another faction?

POLICEMAN

With some pretty bright ideas on how to trap this fiend. It's what we need, isn't it? Different ideas? If one plan fails to achieve results, others crop up. That's natural. Or are you opposed to new ideas?

KLEINMAN

Me? No . . . but they killed Hacker . . .

MAN

Because he wouldn't let go. Because of his dogged insistence that his stupid scheme was the only one. Despite the fact that nothing was happening.

KLEINMAN

So now there are several plans? Or what?

MAN

Right. And I hope you're not married to Hacker's plan. Although plenty still are.

KLEINMAN

I don't even know Hacker's plan.

MAN

Good. Then maybe you can be useful to us.

KLEINMAN

Who's us?

MAN

Don't play innocent.

KLEINMAN

Who's playing?

MAN

Come on.

KLEINMAN

No, I don't know what's going on.

MAN

(Pulls knife on KLEINMAN)
Lives are at stake, you stupid vermin, make your choice.

KLEINMAN

Er . . . officer . . . Constable . . .

POLICEMAN

Now you want help, but last week we were fools because we couldn't catch the killer.

KLEINMAN

No criticism from me.

MAN

Choose, you worm.

POLICEMAN

Nobody gives a damn that we're working around the clock. Snowed under with crackpot confessions. One lunatic after another claiming to be the killer and begging for punishment.

MAN

I've got a good mind to cut your throat, the way you shilly-shally.

KLEINMAN

I'm ready to pitch in. Just tell me what I'm supposed to do.

MAN

Are you with Hacker or with us?

KLEINMAN

Hacker's dead.

MAN

He's got followers. Or maybe you'd rather go along with some splinter group. Eh?

KLEINMAN

If someone would just explain to me what each group stands for. You know what I mean? I never knew Hacker's plan . . . I don't know your plan. I don't know from splinter groups.

MAN

Isn't he the ignorant one, Jack?

POLICEMAN

Yeah. Knows it all until it's time to act. You make me sick.
(The remnants of HACKER'S GROUP enter)

HANK

There you are, Kleinman. Where the hell have you been?

KLEINMAN

Me? Where've you been?

SAM

You wandered off just when we needed you.

KLEINMAN

No one said a word.

MAN

Kleinman's with *us* now.

JOHN

Is that true, Kleinman?

KLEINMAN

Is what true? I don't know what's true any more.
(Several MEN enter. They are an opposing group)

BILL

Hey, Frank. These guys giving you trouble?

FRANK

No. They couldn't if they wanted to.

AL

No?

FRANK

No.

AL

We could have had him trapped already if you boys were where you should have been.

FRANK

We didn't agree with Hacker. His plan wasn't working.

DON

Yeah. We'll catch this killer. Leave it to us.

JOHN

We're not leaving anything to you. Let's go, Kleinman.

FRANK

You're not sticking with them, are you?

KLEINMAN
Me? I'm neutral. Whoever has the best plan.

HENRY
There are no neutrals, Kleinman.

MAN
It's us or them.

KLEINMAN
How can I choose when I don't know the alternatives? Is one apples? Is one pears? Are they both tangerines?

FRANK
Let's kill him now.

SAM
You're not doing any more killing.

FRANK
No?

SAM
No. And when we catch this maniac, someone's going to have to pay for Hacker.

KLEINMAN
While we're standing, arguing, the maniac could be killing someone. The object is to cooperate.

SAM
Tell that to them.

FRANK
Results is the name of the game.

DON
Let's take care of these bastards now. Otherwise they'll stand in our way and confuse the issues.

AL
Just try, big shot.

DEATH

BILL

We'll do more than try.
(Knives and clubs pulled out and brandished)

KLEINMAN

Fellas—boys—

FRANK

Choose now, Kleinman, the moment is here!

HENRY

Better choose right, Kleinman. There's only going to be one winner.

KLEINMAN

We'll kill each other and the maniac'll remain loose. Don't you see? . . . They don't see.
(Fight starts. Suddenly everyone stops and looks up. Winding on stage is an impressive, religious-looking procession that enters, the ASSISTANT leading the way)

ASSISTANT

The murderer! We have located the maniac!
(Fight stops, buzzing, "What's this?" Noise: bong, bong. A group enters with HANS SPIRO, smelling and sniffing)

POLICEMAN

It's Spiro, the telepathic. We've brought him in on the case. He's clairvoyant.

KLEINMAN

Really? He must do well at the race track.

POLICEMAN

He's solved murders for others. All he needs is something to sniff or feel. He read my mind down at headquarters. Knew who I'd just been to bed with.

KLEINMAN

Your wife.

POLICEMAN
(After a dirty look at KLEINMAN)
Look at him, boys. Born with uncanny powers.

ASSISTANT
Mr. Spiro the clairvoyant is on the verge of revealing the killer. Please clear the way. *(SPIRO, working his way, sniffing)* Mr. Spiro wishes to sniff you.

KLEINMAN
Me?

ASSISTANT
Yes.

KLEINMAN
What for?

ASSISTANT
It's enough he wishes it.

KLEINMAN
I don't want to be sniffed.

FRANK
What have you got to hide?
(OTHERS ad-lib agreement)

KLEINMAN
Nothing, but it makes me nervous.

POLICEMAN
Go ahead. Sniff away.
(SPIRO sniffs. KLEINMAN is uncomfortable)

KLEINMAN
What is he doing? I got nothing to hide. My jacket probably smells a little from camphor. Right? Hey, can you stop sniffing me now? It makes me nervous.

AL
Nervous, Kleinman?

KLEINMAN

I never liked getting sniffed. *(SPIRO increases his intensity)* What's the matter? What are you all looking at? What? Oh, I know. I spilled some salad dressing on my pants . . . So there's a faint odor—not too terrible . . . It was the house dressing over at Wilton's Steak House . . . I like steak . . . not rare . . . Well, yes, rare, I mean not raw . . . You know, you order rare and it comes all red?

SPIRO

This man is a murderer.

KLEINMAN

What?

POLICEMAN

Kleinman?

SPIRO

Yes. Kleinman.

POLICEMAN

No!

ASSISTANT

Mr. Spiro has done it again!

KLEINMAN

What are you talking about? Do you know what you're talking about?

SPIRO

Here is the guilty party.

KLEINMAN

You're crazy. Spiro . . . this guy's a lunatic!

HENRY

So, Kleinman, it's been you all along.

FRANK
(Yelling)
Hey—here! Here! We've trapped him!

KLEINMAN
What are you doing?!

SPIRO
There is no doubt. It's conclusive.

BILL
Why'd you do it, Kleinman?

KLEINMAN
Do what? You're going to believe this guy? From smelling me?

ASSISTANT
Mr. Spiro's uncanny power has never failed him yet.

KLEINMAN
This guy's a fake. What's with the smelling!?

SAM
So Kleinman's the murderer.

KLEINMAN
No . . . fellas . . . you all know me!

JOHN
Why'd you do it, Kleinman?

FRANK
Yeah.

AL
He did it because he's crazy. Loco in the head.

KLEINMAN
I'm crazy? Look at the way I'm dressed!

HENRY
Don't expect him to make sense. His mind's gone.

BILL
That's how it is with a crazy man. They can be logical on every point except one—their weakness, their point of insanity.

SAM
And Kleinman's always so damn logical.

HENRY
Too damn logical.

KLEINMAN
This is a joke, right? Because if it's not a joke I'm going to start to cry.

SPIRO
Once again I thank the Lord for the special gift He has seen fit to bestow on me.

JOHN
Let's string him up right now!
(General agreement)

KLEINMAN
Don't come near me! I don't like string!

GINA
(The prostitute)
He tried to attack me! He grabbed me suddenly!

KLEINMAN
I gave you six dollars!
(They grab him)

BILL
I got some rope!

KLEINMAN
What are you doing?

FRANK
We'll make this city safe once and for all.

KLEINMAN
You're hanging the wrong man. I wouldn't hurt a fly . . . okay, a fly maybe—

POLICEMAN
We can't hang him without a trial.

KLEINMAN
Of course not. I have certain rights.

AL
What about the rights of the victims, eh?

KLEINMAN
What victims? I want my lawyer! You hear! I want my lawyer! I don't even have a lawyer!

POLICEMAN
How do you plead, Kleinman?

KLEINMAN
Not guilty. Completely not guilty! I'm not now nor have I ever been a homicidal killer. It doesn't interest me even as a hobby.

HENRY
What have you done to contribute to the capture of the killer?

KLEINMAN
You mean the plan? Nobody told me what it is.

JOHN
Don't you think it's your responsibility to find out for yourself?

KLEINMAN
How? Every time I asked I got a song and dance.

AL
It's your responsibility, Kleinman.

FRANK
That's right. It's not as if there was only one plan.

BILL
Sure. We came up with an alternate plan.

DON
And there were other plans. You could have gotten in on something.

SAM
Is that why you were having trouble choosing? Because you didn't want to choose?

KLEINMAN
Choose between what? Tell me the plan. Let me help. Use me.

POLICEMAN
It's a little late for that.

HENRY
Kleinman, you have been judged and found guilty. You will hang. Do you have any final requests?

KLEINMAN
Yes. I'd prefer not to hang.

HENRY
I'm sorry, Kleinman. There's nothing we can do.

ABE
(Enters in a tizzy)
Quickly—come quickly!

JOHN
What is it?

ABE
We've got the murderer trapped behind the warehouse.

AL
That's impossible. Kleinman's the killer.

ABE
No. He was discovered in the act of strangling Edith Cox. She identified him. Hurry. We need everyone we can get.

SAM
Is it anyone we know?

ABE
No. It's a stranger, but he's on the run!

KLEINMAN
See! See! You were all ready to hang an innocent man.

HENRY
Forgive us, Kleinman.

KLEINMAN
Sure. Anytime you run out of ideas, just drop over with a rope.

SPIRO
There must be some mistake.

KLEINMAN
And you? You ought to have a nose job! *(They all run off)* It's good to know who your friends are. I'm going home! This is no longer my problem! . . . I'm tired, I'm cold . . . some night . . . Now, where am I? . . . Boy, my sense of direction I wouldn't give you two cents for . . . No, that's not right . . . I got to rest a second—get my bearings . . . I'm a little sick from fear . . . *(A noise)* Oh, God . . . now what?

MANIAC
Kleinman?

KLEINMAN
Who are you?

MANIAC

(Who resembles KLEINMAN)

The homicidal killer. Can I sit down? I'm exhausted.

KLEINMAN

What?

MANIAC

Everybody's chasing me . . . I'm running up alleys and in and out of doorways. I'm slinking around town—and they think I'm having fun.

KLEINMAN

You're—the killer?

MANIAC

Sure.

KLEINMAN

I've got to get out of here!

MANIAC

Don't get excited. I'm armed.

KLEINMAN

You—you're going to kill me?

MANIAC

Of course. That's my specialty.

KLEINMAN

You—you're crazy.

MANIAC

Sure I'm crazy. You think a sane person would go around killing people? And I don't even rob them. It's the truth. I never made a penny on a single victim. I never took a pocket comb.

KLEINMAN

So why do you do it?

MANIAC

Why? Because I'm crazy.

KLEINMAN

But you look okay.

MANIAC

You can't go by physical appearance. I'm a maniac.

KLEINMAN

Yeah, but I expected a tall, black, frightening figure . . .

MANIAC

This is not the movies, Kleinman. I'm a man like you. What should I have, fangs?

KLEINMAN

But you've killed so many big, powerful men . . . twice your size . . .

MANIAC

Sure. Because I come up from behind or I wait till they're asleep. Listen, I'm not looking for trouble.

KLEINMAN

But why do you do it?

MANIAC

I'm a screwball. You think I know?

KLEINMAN

Do you like it?

MANIAC

It's not a question of *like*. I do it.

KLEINMAN

But don't you see how ridiculous it is?

MANIAC

If I could see that, I'd be sane.

DEATH

KLEINMAN

How long have you been this way?

MANIAC

As far as I can remember.

KLEINMAN

Can't you be helped?

MANIAC

By who?

KLEINMAN

There's doctors . . . clinics . . .

MANIAC

You think doctors know anything? I been to doctors. I've had blood tests, x-rays. They don't find the craziness. That doesn't show up on an x-ray.

KLEINMAN

What about psychiatry? Mental doctors?

MANIAC

I fool them.

KLEINMAN

Huh?

MANIAC

I act normal. They show me ink blots . . . They ask me if I like girls. I tell 'em sure.

KLEINMAN

This is terrible.

MANIAC

You got any last wishes?

KLEINMAN

You can't be serious!

MANIAC

You wanna hear my crazy laugh?

KLEINMAN

No. Can't you listen to reason? *(MANIAC snaps the switchblade open dramatically)* If you don't get any thrill out of killing me, why do it? It's not logical. You could be using your time constructively . . . Take up golf—be a crazy golfer!

MANIAC

Goodbye, Kleinman!

KLEINMAN

Help! Help! Murder! *(And he's stabbed. The MANIAC runs off)* Ohhh! Ohh!
(A small crowd gathers. We hear: He's dying. KLEINMAN's dying . . . he's dying . . .)

JOHN

Kleinman . . . what was he like?

KLEINMAN

Like me.

JOHN

What do you mean, like you?

KLEINMAN

He looked like me.

JOHN

But Jensen said he looked like Jensen . . . tall and blond, Swedish-looking . . .

KLEINMAN

Oooh . . . You gonna listen to Jensen or you gonna listen to me?

JOHN

All right, don't get angry . . .

DEATH

KLEINMAN

All right, then don't talk like a jerk . . . He looked like me . . .

JOHN

Unless he's a master of disguise . . .

KLEINMAN

Well, he's sure a master of something, and you guys better get on the ball.

JOHN

Bring him some water.

KLEINMAN

What do I need water for?

JOHN

I assumed you were thirsty.

KLEINMAN

Dying doesn't make you thirsty. Unless you get stabbed after eating herring.

JOHN

Are you afraid to die?

KLEINMAN

It's not that I'm afraid to die, I just don't want to be there when it happens.

JOHN
(Musing)
Sooner or later he'll get all of us.

KLEINMAN
(Delirious)
Cooperate . . . God is the only enemy.

JOHN

Poor Kleinman. He's delirious.

KLEINMAN

Oh . . . oh . . . ugggmmmfff.
(Dies)

JOHN

Come on, we've got to come up with a better plan.
(They start going off)

KLEINMAN

(Rises a bare bit)

And another thing. If there is a life after death and we all wind up in the same place—don't call me, I'll call you.
(Expires)

MAN

(Runs on)

The killer's been spotted by the railroad tracks! Come quickly!
(They all go off in pursuit and we
BLACKOUT)

Also By

Woody Allen

ANNIE HALL
DEATH KNOCKS
DON'T DRINK THE WATER
THE FLOATING LIGHT BULB
GOD
INTERIORS
MANHATTAN
OLD SAYBROOK
PLAY IT AGAIN, SAM
RIVERSIDE DRIVE
STARDUST MEMORIES

SAMUELFRENCH.COM

www.ingramcontent.com/pod-product-compliance
Lightning Source LLC
Chambersburg PA
CBHW070650300426
44111CB00013B/2349